*M*any search the earth looking for worldly riches and satisfaction. They do not re-alize that true treasure is found within awaiting the release only they have the power to give. ***Out of the Box–Releasing the Spirit Within*** takes you on a journey of discovery. Robin Anderson provides insight into personal and encountered life experiences that set her spirit free!

As you read ***Out of the Box–Releasing The Spirit Within***, you will have the opportunity to receive, give, or share God's ultimate gift.

— *Robin L. Anderson*

Reviews

"Robin Anderson's *Out of the Box–Releasing the Spirit Within* is an outstanding book filled with spiritual wisdom and insight that will cause you to grow in your relationship with God, conquer your fears and allow God to have full control of his purpose and plan for your life.."

–*Kimberley Brooks,* author of **He's Fine...But is He Saved?**

"An awesome account of one woman's spiritual journey and a wonderful first-person account to finding faith filled with relevant scriptures."...

–*Oralandar Brand-Williams,* Journalist

"Robin Anderson's book on salvation and the rededication of one's life back to the Lord is refreshing and easy to read. *Out of the Box — Releasing the Spirit Within* will compel you to make some changes in your Christian walk."

–*Dr. Janice Hurt-Clarke*

Eva,
God loves you & He has
already set you free. Enjoy the release!

OUT OF THE BOX—

Releasing THE SPIRIT WITHIN

ROBIN L. ANDERSON

Shining Light Works LLC • Farmington, Michigan

Love,
Robin L. Anderson

OUT OF THE BOX - RELEASING THE SPIRIT WITHIN
Published by Robin L. Anderson
Farmington, Michigan

Copyright © 2006 by Robin L. Anderson
International Stanard Book Number 0-9774769-0-1
Library of Congress Catalog Card No: 2006904394

For information, contact:
Shining Light Works, P. O. Box 1072, Farmington, MI 48333
www.shininglightworks.com

All Scripture quotations are taken from the Holy Bible:

King James Version (KJV)

New King James Version (NKJV) - Scripture quotations marked "NKJV™" are taken from the New King James Version®. Copyright©1982 by Thomas Nelson, Inc. Used by permission. All rights reserved.

New International Version (NIV) Scripture taken from the Holy Bible, NEW INTERNATIONAL VERSION®. Copyright© 1973, 1978; 1984 International Bible Society. All rights reserved throughout the world. Used by permission of International Bible Society.

The Living Bible (TLB) - Scripture taken from The Living Bible Copyright © 1971 by Tyndale House Publishers, Wheaton, Illinois 60187. Used by permission of Tyndale House Publishers, Inc. All Rights reserved.

Amplified (AMP) - Scripture taken from THE AMPLIFIED BIBLE, Old Testament copyright© 1965, 1987 by the Zondervan Corporation. The Amplified New Testament copyright© 1958, 1987 By the Lockman Foundation. Used by permission.

Definitions are taken from RANDOM HOUSE WEBSTER'S COLLEGE DICTIONARY. Copyright© 1995, 1992, 1991 by Random House, Inc. Used by permission of Random House, Inc.

Cover & Interior Design: LTerry Design, www.lterrydesign.com
Edited By: Skyla P. Thomas, Pleasant Words

This publication is available at special discount for volume purchasers for sales promotions, premiums, fund-raising or educational use. For details, contact the publisher or visit our web site: www.shininglightworks.com

PRINTED IN THE UNITED STATES OF AMERICA

Dedication

This book is dedicated to GOD.
Your servant has completed the assignment
– to GOD be the glory!

Acknowledgements

I thank God Almighty whose grace and mercy carried me out of the darkness and guided me into the light. You saw beyond my faults to use me as a vessel to convey your message of forgiveness and love. I am eternally grateful for your patience and your marvelous gifts.

I thank God for my earthly support system. To my parents **Robert L.** and **Rosa Anderson**, I am totally thankful and blessed to have you as my parents. Your love and support mean more to me each and every year. I love you dearly.

I thank my brother; **Robert D. Anderson** who I know "has my back". I am blessed to have you in my life.

To my Aunt **Mamie Gattis**, I thank you for your spiritual guidance, love, and support. You have been with me from the beginning of this project. Thanks for "praying" me through.

To my Uncle Al **(Reverend Joseph Blankenship)** thanks for your spiritual presence. I know you are only a call away. You have always been a special blessing to me.

To my cousin **Betty DeVaughn**, "girrrrrl" thanks for your steadfast prayer and Godly example. I just wished I had submitted sooner.

To all my relatives and friends, I thank you for your love, prayers, and support throughout the years. I cherish each and every one of you.

To my spiritual leaders of the *Word of Faith International Christian Center* (WOFICC), **Bishop Keith A. Butler, Pastor Deborah L. Butler, Pastor Keith A. Butler II** and his wife **Minister Tiffany Butler**, I thank you for your obedience to bring forth the Word of God and providing me with "life changing" revelation. Your ministries and the offering of Laypersons and Kingdom Business Institute have fed my spirit, soul, and body.

To **Pastor MiChelle Butler** and **Minister Kristina Butler**, I thank you for blessing me with your ministry gifts.

To **Pastor Joel E. Gregory** and **Minister Patricia Gregory**, thank you for your friendship and support. You are "shining lights" that bring forth the love of God. Pastor Gregory your exemplary leadership as WOFICC Dean of Education led the way for me to receive revelation knowledge and for that I am truly grateful. I appreciate you taking the time to read my book and your favorable response.

To the **WOFICC ministerial staff**, thanks to each of you for your unique spiritual gifts and ministries, you continue to bless and enrich my life.

Bishop Andrew and **Pastor Viveca Merritt** of *Straight Gate Church*, I thank you for offering the Catechism curriculum. Catechism provided a door for my hunger to know more about the things of God. I appreciate you and the awesome instructors who made such a wonderful impact on my life.

Dr. Patricia Beall Gruits, teacher of God's Word and the author of *"Understanding God and His Covenants"* and *"Understanding the Master's Voice"*, I thank you for your obedience to God that led you to teach Catechism at Straight Gate Church. To have the instructor of the textbook as the teacher of the class was extremely gratifying. Your insight and wisdom continues to bless me today.

I acknowledge the following people for their expertise and help in bringing this project to light:

To my spiritual mentors **Dr. Victor Eagan** and **Minister Catherine Eagan**, *Kingdom Business Institute* leaders and authors of *"How to Discover your Purpose in 10 Days"*, your awesome gifts and heart for revealing the purpose of God's people have blessed my life as well as many others worldwide. Thanks for providing Godly wisdom and warning me not to move forward without the proper foundation. Minister Eagan, your coaching was instrumental towards the breakthrough for completing this book.

To **Pastor Donna Stallings** *(It's Your Time Ministries)*, I thank you for caring enough to let God work through you to minister to me. You were part of my rebirth and for that I am eternally grateful. Your global ministry to women is definitely a Godsend. I thank you for being a part of my Christian walk and for being a part of my life.

Thanks to the following ministries for blessing my life and for your steadfast prayers: **Grace Is Sufficient Ministries,** *(Minister Julie Jackson-Ward, Minister Rochelle Duncan)* and **Eagle International Bible Training Center,** *(Minister Carlene Lucas);* **Children of Destiny International** *(Pastor Briggie Stansberry-Beater).*

Leanelle Simmons, thank you for being available with a listening ear and a helping hand during the completion of this book. Your support and friendship are a gift from God.

Dr. Janice Hurt-Clarke, thank you for utilizing your proof reading skills. I can always count on you. I am blessed to have your life-long friendship and support.

LaTanya Orr of *LTerry Design,* thanks for your extraordinary efforts to bring this book to life. You have been such a blessing. God sends us those special people to help us produce His will. I thank God for sending you. Your creative talents are evident from the cover of the book to the inside format. God has truly provided you with marvelous gifts. Thank you for your willingness to share your gifts and knowledge with others.

Skyla Thomas of *Pleasant Words,* I thank you for your editing skills. You have a gift for editing words and sentence structure without changing the message. Thank you for helping me create a concise and easy to read work.

Pam Perry of *Ministry Marketing Solutions,* your information and guidance has been a blessing in bringing forth this vision.

To **Tracy Flaggs,** author of *"In the Eye of the Storm"*, I believe our meeting was divinely led of God. Thank you for sharing your awesome testimony through your book. I thank you for all of your help and inspiring me to bring forth God's assignment.

To **Kimberley Brooks**, author of *"He's Fine, But is He Saved"*, you are most definitely a woman of virtue. You have been very helpful to this novice writer. Thanks for sharing the invaluable information and your experiences to self-publishing.

Kimberly Benjamin, author of *"How to be Highly Favored and Empowered to Prosper in Your Job Search"*, thanks for taking the time to share and answer questions about your experiences in writing. God's blessings to you as you walk in your purpose.

Oralandar Brand-Williams, thank you for endorsing my manuscript. I truly value your positive review as a professional journalist.

Kate McVeigh, I appreciate you reading my manuscript despite your hectic schedule. Your encouraging response means a lot.

Dr. Byron Douglas, thanks for taking the time to read my manuscript. I truly appreciate the positive feedback.

To **Michelle Jefferson**, make-up artist and hair stylist, thanks for making me "camera ready" for the author's photo. I believe our meeting and re-introduction was in God's plan. Your prayers directed me to my current church home.

To **Glenn Corcoran**, photographer and owner of *The Photo Center*, thank you for your talents in providing the author's photo.

Dornique Jefferson of *Advancing Business Technologies*, thank you for your creativity and design of my website **www.shininglightworks.com**.

Bridghette Parker, thank you for your finishing touch in bringing this book to completion.

To **all of you reading this book**, I pray that you receive a spiritual release, accept God's greatest gift, and share the message.

Table of Contents

Introduction

Introduction

Have you ever received a gift and thought the package was too pretty to open? The package was meticulously wrapped and the paper covering the box was exquisite. The fabric of the bow was attractive and knotted to perfection. The outside of the box was appealing to the eye and could itself be considered a work of art. Just imagine if you left the gift wrapped and unopened. The wrapping would eventually become faded, tattered, and frayed from exposure. That once beautifully wrapped package would no longer appear beautiful and the most valued part (the gift inside the box) would remain unknown. How tragic to miss out on the true gift. Many people walk around appearing to have it all together on the outside, yet inside they feel inadequate and unfulfilled. God has a gift for you! Open your gift, the gift God has placed inside each of us. Take your gift *Out of the Box – Releasing the Spirit Within.*

James 1:17 KJV - Every good gift and every perfect gift is from above and cometh down from the Father of lights, with whom is no variableness, neither shadow of turning.

Chapter One

Beauty's More than Skin-Deep

hat is beauty? Webster describes beauty as "the quality present in a person or thing that gives intense aesthetic pleasure or deep satisfaction to the mind or senses." Most people think of beauty from the world's perspective - "skin-deep" beauty, the outer appearance. To view beauty as skin deep is being superficial. According to Webster's dictionary, the definition of "superficial is being at, on, or near the surface; external or outward; apparent rather than real; concerned with or comprehending only what is on the surface or obvious; shallow - not profound or thorough; insubstantial or insignificant."

My ideas of beauty originated like that of most – beauty based on exposure and perception: Exposure to the media (television, magazines, etc.) and the perceptions of my peers. Everyone wants to be liked and accepted. Unfortunately, most want to be liked or accepted by the "wrong" people. The "wrong" people are the people who look at things and life in the wrong way - the "skin-deep" way. They totally miss out on real beauty, the beauty hidden within.

2 Corinthians 4:18 KJV - While we look not at the things which are seen, but at the things which are not seen: for the things which are seen are temporal; but the things which are not seen are eternal.

People, especially children can be extremely cruel to those who "appear" different. We can all refer to our childhood when someone was singled out from the group for not fitting in or for being of a different weight, wearing different clothing, having different hair, speaking differently, or for just being different. Usually there was a ringleader, the bully who led the group by instigating cruelty on the ostracized child. The ringleader was the person the group looked up to and esteemed for reasons which seemed important at the time, but looking back you wonder why the group valued their opinions and honored them with authority. No one dared to speak out in defense of the ostracized child for fear of retaliation from the ringleader or the entire group. And besides, you wanted to "fit in." So most joined in on the cruelty to be part of the crowd or stood in silence while the others jeered. Unfortunately, this elitist attitude can also be observed in adults. People ostracize others from organizations, friendships, and even families.

Matthew 26:67-75 NKJV - Then they spat in His face and beat Him; and others struck Him with the palms of their hands, saying, "Prophesy to us, Christ! Who is the one who struck You?" Now Peter sat outside in the courtyard. And a servant girl came to him, saying, "You also were with Jesus of Galilee." But he denied it before them all, saying, "I do not know what you are saying." And when he had gone out to the gateway, another girl saw him and said to those who were there, "This fellow also was with Jesus of Nazareth." But again he denied with an oath, "I do not know the Man!" And a little later those who stood by came up and said to Peter, "Surely you also are one of them, for your speech betrays you." Then he began to curse and swear, saying, "I do not know the Man!" Immediately a rooster crowed. And Peter remembered the word of Jesus who had said to him, "Before the rooster crows, you will deny Me three times." So he went out and wept bitterly.

Be careful who you give authority to over your life!

Girls begin to focus on their outer appearance at an early age. In fact, for some, it's a very sensitive area. "What should I wear?" "I'm too fat!" "I'm too skinny!" They never quite fit into the "perfect" scenario

– the scenario they have conjured in their mind to fulfill. Perfection is sought from an imperfect world. The world that looks at external beauty often times neglects the qualities of a person that lie within.

I Peter 3: 3,4 NIV - Your beauty should not come from outward adornment, such as braided hair and the wearing of gold jewelry and fine clothes. Instead, it should be that of your inner self, the unfading beauty of a gentle and quiet spirit, which is of great worth in God's sight.

This does not mean that you should neglect your outer appearance. Our bodies are the temples of God. We must present our outer and inner selves at our best. We have God in us. We do not have to lavish our bodies with expensive clothing, however, we need to be well groomed – well groomed on the outside and on the inside. Just like we take care of our outer bodies with daily cleansing, we must keep the inner body cleansed with the daily reading and washing with God's Word.

Some young girls and women think of beauty from the opposite sex's point of view. Idol status is placed on those females who have appealing physical characteristics – those who have the "right" look and are the "right" size. These girls have "it" all together. Right? Wrong!

Proverbs 31:30 AMP - Charm and grace are deceptive, and beauty is vain [because it is not lasting], but a woman who reverently and worshipfully fears the Lord, she shall be praised!

Besides, a lot of the "it" girls have their own insecurities. "Do I have anything to offer besides a pretty face?" "Does he really care for me or my double-D attributes?" "I have to constantly prove my value as a competent person."

Some females are misled and want the attraction of the entire male gender, not realizing that their real desire is for just one man, the right man appointed for her by God as her mate. It only takes the love of one man, not the admiration of many. Other females want the attraction of men, but selfishly want their independence. They don't need anyone or anybody. They want to do their own thing and answer to no one! While other sisters want the attention of men, but don't want to admit it. "I don't need, want, or care about a man." Secretly fearing rejection, they feel they don't measure up to the world's beauty standards.

A lot of unpleasant experiences could be avoided or minimized if people did not determine their worth by the presence or absence of having someone on their arm. Some have gone through physical, mental, or self abuse because they are unaware of their worth as a person. Through God's Word and His love, you will not tolerate being treated any kind of way, being disrespected, or disrespect yourself. If you take the time to know who you are and better still, whose you are (God's), you will realize your true value.

1 Corinthians 6: 19-20 AMP - Do you not know that your body is the temple (the very sanctuary) of the Holy Spirit Who lives within you. Whom you have received [as a Gift] from God? You are not your own. You were bought with a price [purchased with a preciousness and paid for, made His own]. So then, honor God and bring glory to Him in your body.

Proverbs 31: 10 AMP - A capable, intelligent, and virtuous woman - who is he who can find her? She is far more precious than jewels and her value is far above rubies or pearls.

The truly blessed sisters know or come to realize that the world's skin-deep idea of beauty is superficial and is not the right idea of beauty. We are all beautiful in the eyes of God. The real beauty of a person is hidden within and when you take the time to know the inner person, the true essence (spirit) of the person is revealed.

1 Samuel 16:7 NKJV - But the Lord said to Samuel, "Do not look at his appearance or at his physical stature, because I have refused him. For the Lord does not see as man sees; for man looks at the outer appearance, but the Lord looks at the heart."

Chapter Two
Let Go and
Let God

One day my world came crashing in. Until that time, I pretty much had control over my life or at least I thought I did. The inner turmoil was tucked neatly away from the public's view. My career, my relationships and my "Buppie" (Black Urban Professional) status was intact. Suddenly, I lost my self-imposed control. Like Humpty Dumpty, everything came tumbling down. The loss of control triggered a physical eruption. All the years of inner hurt and pain that I had hidden away came to the surface. My face began to erupt with bumps, lesions, and sores. I would attempt to cover the "imperfections" with make-up. But, after a while, I could not hide behind the make-up any longer. I sought help from a dermatologist. When the dermatologist saw my face, she asked what I was doing and what was I putting on my face. The doctor also asked what I was eating and what medications was I ingesting. There was no medical explanation to why this facial eruption had happened. I was diagnosed with severe acute acne. It wasn't what I was putting on my face or in my body, but it was what was coming out of my body. The loss of self-control resulted in my inner emotions taking over my physical body.

The dermatologist stated that in order for my face to heal I should take off the make-up. Take off the make-up! I couldn't comprehend. Exposing this ugly mess to the world. Already insecure about my looks prior to this episode, it took all I had to go without make-up. Even though at this point I was only hiding the discoloration of my skin, not it's unhealthy texture. When the make-up came off, I experienced cruelty, verbal abuse, and humiliation. During this period I still attempted to keep my emotions in check. I went about my daily routine through taunts, snickers behind my back, and rude remarks to my face. But, even more hurting than the rude words were the stares. There's one experience that I will never forget. It happened while I was shopping at a store. A lady in the store had a little boy with her. She looked at me with horror as she grabbed the little boy out of the way as though she was trying to protect him from some kind of contagious disease. The sad thing is I could not blame her. I would have probably done the same thing if I had been in her shoes. I felt like a disfigured animal!

I would still follow my Sunday ritual of going to church. Instead of my usual seating area in the balcony, I found a new hiding place in the basement of the church to sit. The church basement was usually reserved for overflow crowds on special occasions, or as a place where people went when they were late for service and didn't want to be seen, or had unruly children. In the church basement the service could be viewed on a screen. I've always had compassion for others, however this experience humbled me and made me even more accepting of other people.

When people are under stress, it affects their nervous system. Stressful environments often manifest into harmful bodily diseases. I am grateful that my body reacted with a non-terminal physical condition. It was only by the grace and mercy of God that the severe acne did not cause permanent scarring. A young lady recently who was not comfortable with her looks admiringly made the comment to me, "Not everyone can look like you." I thought to myself, 'If she only knew me back then.' People look at the outside never realizing an individual's life experiences and what they go through. Some even desire to trade places with other people based on outer appearances and viewed circumstances not taking into consideration the exchange. You don't know that person or what their life is really like. Remember the old saying – be careful of what you ask for, you just might get it! The ordeal with my skin could have been avoided. Our bodies were not made to bear all of our burdens. When we continue to take burdens in and hold on to them, it is only a matter of time before our burdens turn into health challenges. Our Heavenly Father waits on us to hand our burdens over to Him. Let go and let God!

Psalm 55:22 AMP - Cast your burden on the Lord [releasing the weight of it] and He will sustain you; He will never allow the [consistently] righteous to be moved (made to slip, fall, or fail).

Clean out your house! We hold on to clutter, trash, and other worthless stuff unconsciously claiming the stuff as our own. Go into your inner closet and release the issues of your past -- old hurts, disappointments, and people who have mistreated you. We are so quick to blame others for our circumstances, but we need to examine ourselves to see if we had a role to play in the occurrence. People cannot hurt you if you don't let them. By holding onto grudges, you allow the person that hurt you to continue to do so. They have gone on with their lives and you are left carrying old baggage. Get a new lease on life! You seek forgiveness from the Lord, but who haven't you forgiven? How do you expect God to forgive you of your sins when you haven't forgiven others of their sins against you? Look at Jesus! They spat on Him, beat Him, and they crucified Him. In spite of all this, Jesus asked God to forgive those who harmed Him. If Jesus, who was without sin can forgive, who are we to hold on to grudges?

Luke 23:32-34 NKJV - There were also two others, criminals, led with Him to be put to death. And when they had come to the place called Calvary, there they crucified Him, and the criminals, one on the right hand and the other on the left. Then Jesus said, "Father, forgive them, for they do not know what they do." And they divided His garments and cast lots.

Mark 11:25-26 AMP - And whenever you stand praying, if you have anything against anyone, forgive him and let it drop (leave it, let it go), in order that your Father Who is in heaven may also forgive you your [own] failings and shortcomings and let them drop. But if you do not forgive, neither will your Father in heaven forgive your failings and shortcomings.

While you are forgiving others, don't forget to forgive yourself. At times we blame ourselves for causing or allowing situations to happen. You may have some wounds that are too deep for you to forgive yourself or others on your own. But, with Jesus as the head of your life nothing is impossible. Jesus is our comforter, healer, deliverer, and our help. This doesn't mean that with God in your life you will never encounter trouble, sorrow, or disappointments. However when trouble, sorrow, or disappointment arrives, God will see you through your storm.

John 16:33 AMP - I have told you these things, so

11

that in Me you may have [perfect] peace and
confidence. In the world you have tribulation and
trials and distress and frustration; but be of good cheer
[take courage; be confident, certain, undaunted]! For I
have overcome the world. [I have deprived it of power
to harm you and have conquered it for you.]

Give your burdens to the Lord. With God's gift of
salvation you will receive a new heart. You will experience a rebirth (a spiritual birth) and become a new
creature. You can receive a peace beyond all understanding. Joy can replace sadness. A smile can replace
a frown. I laugh when I think back to a time when I
walked around with a scowl on my face – always looking unhappy. I was unaware of it until other people
would ask me why I wasn't smiling. I would comment,
"People would think I was crazy if I walked around
smiling for no reason." Now, most days I walk around
with a pleasant demeanor. Now people ask me what I
am smiling about. When I think about the goodness
of God, how can I not smile?

Chapter Three

The Spiritual Journey

I've spent the majority of my life going to church. I wish that I could say that my church life has always been spiritual, but for the most part it was a Sunday ritual. A ritual is defined by Webster as "Any practice or pattern of behavior regularly performed in a set manner. An established procedure for a religious or other rite." I had spent over twenty years going through the motions of attending church, but not really open to giving and receiving true worship.

Galatians 3:2 AMP – Let me ask you this one question: Did you receive the [Holy] Spirit as the result of obeying the Law and doing its works, or was it by hearing [the message of the Gospel] and believing [it]? [Was it from observing a law of rituals or from a message of faith?]

"Good girls" obey their parents and go to church on Sundays. My earliest memories of church is going to Sunday school, coloring biblical pictures and singing songs like "Yes Jesus Loves Me." But, I really didn't know the extent to what that meant. It would be years before I would comprehend just how much Jesus loved me. Jesus loves you and me so much that He was willing to sacrifice His own life to wash away our sins.

1 John 2:1-2 AMP – My Little children, I write you these things so that you may not violate God's law and sin. But if anyone should sin, we have an Advocate (One Who will intercede for us) with the Father – [it is] Jesus Christ [the all] righteous [upright, just, Who conforms to the Father's will in every purpose, thought, and action]. And He [that same Jesus Himself] is the propitiation (the atoning sacrifice) for our sins, and not for ours alone but also for [the sins of] the whole world.

As a child I attended Catholic, Methodist, and Baptist churches. My first baptism was in a Methodist church. The Methodist baptism consisted of being sprinkled with water. I attended the Methodist church through my High school and college years. During my college years, I only attended church when I came home from school on weekends and holidays. While I was away at school,

I never attended church service. However, I maintained my rituals of saying grace before I ate (except in public settings) and my prayers before I went to bed. I would not say grace in public settings because I was too afraid of what people would think. I never saw other people saying grace in restaurants. The Lord's Prayer was my evening prayer before retiring for bed. My nightly prayer would end with special prayers for someone else or for something I felt I needed or wanted. I would go through the same prayer rituals every day and night.

With a Biochemistry undergraduate degree, I took many science courses during my college years. I remember one course in particular when an instructor was lecturing on the subject of Darwin's Theory of Evolution and how man evolved from apes. At the time I questioned God's existence and wondered how I was supposed to believe in something I could not see. The instructor then began lecturing that human life was the result of the "Big Bang Theory." The "Big Bang Theory" proposes that a cosmic explosion took place in space and propelled dense matter to form the universe. All life forms evolved from the particles of that explosion. Scientific theories have not been able to answer the questions, who initiated the first form of life or formed the dense matter that exploded in space. Was there anyone there to witness these occurrences firsthand? No one can explain all the details of Darwin's Theory of Evolution, the Big Bang Theory, or other less accepted origin of life hypotheses.

However scholars and atheists worldwide, accept these ideas as fact for the explanation of life's origin. People are quick to believe that human life resulted from an explosion or evolved from some other life form. Why not believe in God? Some refuse to believe that a being greater than them was responsible for creating life.

> **Genesis 1:1 KJV** – In the beginning God created the heaven and the earth.

> **Psalm 8:3 KJV** – When I consider thy heavens, the work of thy fingers, the moon and the stars, which thou hast ordained;

> **Genesis 2:7 KJV** – And the Lord God formed man of the dust of the ground, and breathed into his nostrils the breath of life; and man became a living soul.

Who is God? God is love (I John 4:8). You can't touch or see love, but love exists. You may shower someone with love by doing the things that make the person happy. A parent loves their children by sheltering, feeding, clothing, and protecting them. Love takes on many forms. Although we see manifestations of love and not a physical substance or form, no one doubts love exists. At times it is difficult to believe in something or someone that we cannot see. Microscopes, binoculars, voltmeters, ultrasounds, x-rays, and other visual aids allow the capability to see things that appear invisible with our natural eyesight (i.e. sound waves, electricity). These visual aids provide evidence for things that may seemingly appear invisible, but upon closer examination are found to actually exist.

Colossians 1:16 NIV – For by him all things were created: things in heaven and on earth, visible and invisible, whether thrones or powers or rulers or authorities; all things were created by him and for him.

John 20:24-29 KJV – But Thomas, one of the twelve, called Didymus, was not with them when Jesus came. The other disciples therefore said unto him, We have seen the Lord. But he said unto them, Except I shall see in his hands the print of the nails, and put my finger into the print of the nails, and thrust my hand into his side, I will not believe. And after eight days again his disciples were within, and Thomas with them: then came Jesus, the doors being shut, and stood in the midst, and said, Peace be unto you. Then saith he to Thomas, Reach hither thy finger, and behold my hands; and reach hither thy hand, and thrust it into my side: and be not faithless, but believing. And Thomas answered and said unto him, My Lord and my God. Jesus saith unto him, Thomas, because thou hast seen me, thou hast believed: blessed are they that have not seen, and yet have believed.

God's manifestations of love are all around us. God created all things visible and invisible: the air that we breathe, the beauty of the trees, the flowers, the grass, the heavens, the moon and the stars, the sun, the waters and the mountains, the various species of life, and man. God has designed the intricate details of man and all living things (i.e. reproduction, birth). Can anyone believe that life is a haphazard occurrence that came about without a plan? Discover for yourself if God exists. You will find God when you search for Him with an open heart.

Jeremiah 29:13 NIV – You will seek me and find me when you seek me with all your heart.

After graduating from college I returned to my parents' home while I began to look for a job. I began regular attendance at the Methodist church of my youth and picked up "spiritually" where I left off as a pew member. For those who don't know, a pew member is someone who attends church but is not actively involved in the church (i.e. choir, usher, committee member, etc.). Although I was not active in the church, I rarely missed attending Sunday church services. It was around this time that I began to search for a new church home, partly to fulfill an unmet spiritual need and partly to proclaim my independence. Attending a Pentecostal or Spirit-filled church was definitely not a consideration. I thought I was too prim and proper for that type of worship. I remember talking with some of my college-graduated girl-friends who were equally, if not more prim and proper than I. The "girls" decided, "It does not take all of that" when speaking about enthusiastic worship to God. Many people tolerate those who faint and pass out over rock stars or scream and yell until they lose their voices when a player hits or throws a ball, but expect solemn tribute when it comes to worshipping God. It is strange how the world accepts adulation and wild actions when it comes to fans showing their love and appreciation for sports heroes and entertainers, however, high-spirited outward expressions toward God are thought by many as extreme. I am not saying that it is mandatory for all to scream, yell, run around the church, or roll on the floor to praise the Lord, however some have experienced their biggest breakthroughs by this type of exuberant praise and worship.

> 2 Samuel 6:14-16, 21 AMP - And David danced before the Lord with all his might, clad in a linen ephod [a priest's upper garment]. So David and all the house of Israel brought up the ark of the Lord with shouting and with the sound of the trumpet. As the ark of the Lord came into the City of David, Michal, Saul's daughter [David's wife], looked out of the window and saw King David leaping and dancing before the Lord, and she despised him in her heart.
>
> David said to Michal, It was before the Lord, Who

chose me above your father and all his house to
appoint me as prince over Israel, the people of
the Lord. Therefore will I make merry
[in pure enjoyment] before the Lord.

Psalm 98:4 KJV – Make a joyful noise unto
the Lord, all the earth: make a loud noise,
and rejoice, and sing praise.

There is more than one way to honor God. Less expressive forms of worship also please Him.

Exodus 4:31 NIV – and they believed. And when
they heard that the Lord was concerned about
them and had seen their misery, they bowed
down and worshipped.

No one should dictate or judge how someone else is
led to worship God. A person's relationship with God
and their method of worshipping Him are between
God and that person.

I began visiting a friend's Baptist church. I enjoyed the
services at the church. The minister was charismatic and
his sermons were eloquent. At times I would feel as
though the minister's message was directed at me. The
church service was more upbeat than my previous place
of worship. One Sunday I went down to the altar to join
the Baptist church. I remember the clerk asking if I had

been baptized. I told him that I was baptized at a Methodist church by being sprinkled with water. The clerk responded that I would need to be baptized again. The Baptist baptism involved total submerging of the body under water. I was always terribly afraid of putting my head under water due to a tragic incident that had happened to a classmate during my youth. My first thought of being baptized again was the fear of putting my head under water. My second thought was that I did not see a need to be baptized again since I had already been baptized (sprinkled with water) and believed in God. However, I went through with the second baptism although my thought was, 'This is something I am doing to fulfill the criteria for joining the Baptist church.' Although my heart was not fully prepared for the baptism experience, I fulfilled the obligation and was now officially part of the Baptist church. My supervisor at work gave me a book on what Baptist's believe. I read the book and didn't see a lot of differences from what the Methodists believe except for the act of water baptism. The Bible details the following concerning Jesus' water baptism:

Mark 1: 9-10 NIV – At that time Jesus came from Nazareth in Galilee and was baptized by John in the Jordan. As Jesus was coming up out of the water, he saw heaven being torn open and the Spirit descending on him like a dove.

My friend always sat in the balcony at the Baptist church and I would sit in the balcony with her. I remember asking her why she sat in the balcony and she told me that the view was better. So, I continued to sit in the balcony too. Besides, I did not feel comfortable with the large size of the Baptist church and sitting in the balcony distanced me from the majority of the congregation. The Baptist church's membership was more than three times the size of the Methodist church I had attended. I made the Baptist church my church home for fourteen years. At the Baptist church I continued the pew member role that I had at the Methodist church. One day I decided to attend a Women's group meeting at the church with the intent of joining. The Women's group met on Saturdays and at that time I was required to work some Saturdays. So, the next few Saturdays I was unable to attend the Women's group meetings. The leader from the Women's group called to inquire about my lack of attendance and I explained to her that I could not attend because I had to work. The group leader had a real attitude on the phone as though she thought I was not being truthful. After that conversation, I was turned off from joining any group in the church especially if that was the attitude of the leaders. However, I volunteered my services one week out of the year during Christian Education week. And, I continued to attend church services faithfully.

Years ago, one of my cousins who lives in another state and is about 10 years older than me had become "saved." I had always admired this cousin. I thought she was very attractive and fashionable. My cousin came to Detroit for a visit and had totally changed. Being worldly however, I could mostly detect the change in her outward appearance. This once attractive and fashionable person who I admired, stopped wearing make-up including lipstick, and started wearing loose fitting long dresses and skirts (which were not fashionable at that time). During those years, the "saved" women and evangelists were dressed less than fashionable and definitely did not wear make-up. Make-up for "saved" women at that time was considered taboo! My cousin would invite me to go to different sanctified churches with her whenever she was in town. She would say "Girrrrl, you don't know what you are missing." My thought was "Girrrrl, I don't know and I don't want to know. If being "saved" did that to you, there is no way that I'm going with you." I would always pass on her invitation. Fortunately, she didn't know what I was really thinking. I now realize I was being judgmental by looking at the outer her and missing out on the new inner her. Besides that, I was missing out on my own blessing. But, at that time I did not feel that I needed to be "saved." "Saved" from what? After all, although I was not a saint, by the world's standards I was a "good" and honest person. I believed in God, I went to church on Sundays. I did not smoke and would rarely drink or use profanity. I did not gamble or cause my parents pain, and I was always reaching out to help others. I had a professional career, I worked hard, I had both Bachelor's and Master's degrees. I had a new car, and I had just purchased a condominium. I had traveled extensively, both domestically and abroad, and had taken up skiing and golf (although, I was not good at either). If you had asked most people about my character they would have only positive things to say. Why did I need to be "saved"? I was living the American dream!

Jeremiah 9: 23-24 AMP – Thus says the Lord: Let not the wise and skillful person glory and boast in his wisdom and skill; let not the mighty and powerful person glory and boast in his strength and power; let not the person who is rich [in physical gratification and earthly wealth] glory and boast in his [temporal satisfactions and earthly] riches; But let him who glories glory in this: that he understands and knows Me [personally and practically, directly discerning and recognizing My character], that I am the Lord, Who practices loving-kindness, judgment, and righteousness in the earth, for in these things I delight, says the Lord.

My plans had been fulfilled for the most part. But now what? What was next? With all I felt I had accomplished, there was still a void in my life. Something was missing and I couldn't put my finger on it. I only knew that more money, more degrees, or more stuff was not going to fill the void. Now, with the majority of my dreams fulfilled,

I began to feel empty. Even more than feeling empty, I began to "feel dead on the inside." I didn't know at that time that the death I was experiencing was a spiritual death. I had accomplished my goals, however I wasn't happy. During this time God sent me a spiritual mentor. I had known "Lady D" at work only in passing. We would always say hello and make small talk. But for some reason our conversations turned more spiritual. Unknown to me, "Lady D" was an evangelist. One day she asked me if I was saved. I thought for a moment, and then answered, "I guess I'm saved." I did not see why I wouldn't be saved since I was not a bad person. But, I was not sure. I had many questions about God amidst my strong independent spirit. Lady D suggested that I take a catechism course. "Catechism", I said out loud. "Isn't that a class for Catholics?" Lady D explained that Catechism is an in-depth study of the Bible. She stated that through the Catechism class and prayer I would receive answers to my many questions. I found a Catechism class at a Pentecostal church. The class was truly a blessing. It was during that class that I prayed to God to reveal to me the church that He wanted me to attend.

When you ask God for revelation and expect Him to answer, He may answer you in indirect ways. Initially, God started placing new people in my path who attended my current church home. I thought it a little strange that every person that I was meeting attended the same church, but since the church membership is so large, I thought it must be coincidental. Then one night after praying, God revealed to me a church building that I had never seen before. Unknown to me, this would be the new sanctuary for my current church home. At first I was in denial. God couldn't mean for me to attend "that church." The church was even larger than my Baptist church home. Besides, I did not know if I was ready for that "type" of worship. I had heard rumors about "that church." I began the search for my new church home by attending different churches of various faiths. One week I would attend my Baptist church, the next I would visit a different church, all along keeping the church that the Lord revealed to me in the back of my mind. One church that I had visited had a dress code for those attending worship services or classes in the sanctuary. Women had to wear skirts and dresses and men were required to wear shirts with ties. I wondered how many lost souls slipped through the cracks while this church turned some away based upon their clothing and outer appearance. You never know where someone's heart is when he or she initially turns up at the church door. Perhaps they did not have time to go home and change clothing or maybe they were so distraught that they did not consider what they were wearing. Maybe if someone from the church would have approached them in love to find out what their specific situation was before they turned them away, it may have saved that person's life.

Eventually, I reluctantly visited my current church home. Although I enjoyed the service, I was not ready to join. I wanted to make sure that this was indeed the place God wanted me to be. I did not want to be out of His will. In actuality, it took some time for me to convince myself that God really wanted me at "that church." It would be about six months before I was certain that I should leave the Baptist church. It was not an easy decision since I had regularly attended services at the Baptist church for fourteen years. But, one Sunday I attended the Baptist church service and I knew it was time for me to leave. My spirit let me know that I could no longer stay. The Sunday that I joined my current church, I arrived very late. Usually anyone arriving that late would surely end up sitting at the back of the church. But, as soon as I arrived, it was as though God had prepared the way. Ushers one-by-one beckoned me forward as I approached their respective area, until I was seated at the end of the second row of the center aisle. God had set it up so that when the call was brought forth for those who wanted to join the church, I was the first person to arrive at the alter. My new church home has truly been a blessing. I have learned so much and I continue to grow spiritually. When you are obedient to God's direction, He will lead you to exactly where you should be.

Chapter Four
Why Am I Afraid?

I is ironic how some things we should fear we don't, and some things we fear we should embrace. Fear is the opposite of faith. Webster defines faith as "confidence or trust in a person or thing." And, fear is defined as "a distressing emotion aroused by impending danger, evil, pain, etc., whether the threat is real or imagined." God is the messenger of faith and Satan is the messenger of fear. Satan's mission is to steal, kill, and destroy. Therefore, building faith is essential. Faith comes from knowing and hearing the Word of God (Romans 10:17).

Throughout the Bible, God's Word gives us examples of people and situations to guide us and teach us lessons to prevent us from going through unpleasant experiences. One such example is Lot's wife. The Word of God never mentions the name of Lot's wife. The name of Lot's wife is insignificant. However in Luke 17:32, God warns us to "Remember Lot's wife!" I believe God wants us to remember her, her lack of faith, and the result of her disobedience.

In Genesis 19, God sent angels to help Lot and his family escape destruction. They were to be shown the way to the Promised Land, but were warned not to look back. Lot's wife however looked back and became a pillar of salt. If Lot's wife was going to the Promised Land, why did she feel the need to look back? Did she fear and lack faith? Lot's wife was familiar with the life she was leaving behind with all its entrapments and her possessions. And even though sin was rampant in the town and the townspeople, Lot's wife did not want to release her past. Perhaps, she did not trust the untraveled territory that was before her. She may have not trusted that what God had in store for her was far better than her past. Maybe she felt the comfort of the known was better than the uncertainty of the unknown. Whatever the reason for the disobedience, the cost was her life. Lot's wife became a pillar of salt, a reminder, and a monument that resulted from disobedience. The symbol of Lot's wife as a pillar of salt sends a lesson to those who are afraid to let go of the past – holding on to the familiar even when it is not good for you to do so. Holding on to the past stops you dead in your tracks. You cease to make progress in that area of your life. Fear paralyzes you and can destroy you. Like the pillar of salt, it will harden your interior (your heart) as well as you exterior (your demeanor). Fear and the lack of faith prevent you from receiving the blessings that God has for you. What is encompassing you? What is your salt? What has stopped you from moving forward? Fear not! Let the past go and move forward into your purpose.

You will experience pain whether you hold on to the pain or deal with the pain and release it. The difference between the two is whether you keep it as a monument (a reminder) of what you went through and let the pain continue to rule your life or release the pain, grow from the experience, and move forward. Don't let your life become a monument of your pain. Your past pain can become your future testimony! God can show you a way out from your pain if you are willing to turn away from it. Stop blaming Satan or someone else for your lack of progress. Satan only puts up the roadblocks, we determine the paths that we choose. Release your fears and move in faith towards God's plan for your life.

Jeremiah 29:11 NIV - For I know the plans I have for you, declares the Lord, plans to prosper you and not to harm you, plans to give you hope and a future.

One of my most rewarding life experiences came by releasing fear and receiving in faith the gift of "speaking in tongues." I had a very difficult time receiving this gift from God and developing open communication with the Holy Spirit. Just like any gift, in order to benefit and enjoy it you have to accept it. The giver of the gift makes the gift available and the receiver of the gift has the option to receive or reject it.

Luke 11: 9-10, 13 KJV - And I say unto you, Ask, and it shall be given you; seek, and ye shall find; knock, and it shall be opened unto you. For everyone that asketh receiveth; and he that seeketh findeth; and to him that knocketh it shall be opened.
If ye then, being evil, know how to give good gifts unto your children: how much more shall your heavenly Father give the Holy Spirit to them that ask him?

The first time that "tongues" came upon me was years ago as I was awakened from my sleep. It was a very strange experience. I knew that people spoke in tongues but I had no real understanding of what it meant and I must admit I even wondered if some people were faking. Well, since it happened to me I believed that "tongues" was real, but I still didn't understand it. My personal experience made me a believer of the act only.

The second time I spoke in tongues was years later. One evening, the Lord led me to call Lady D on her cell phone. At the time of my call, she was in a meeting with some fellow evangelists. I told her that I was interested in receiving the Baptism of the Holy Spirit, based upon our previous conversations. She encouraged me to meet with her and her fellow evangelists. Upon my arrival, the evangelists encircled me. "What if nothing happens?" I asked them. "I am a very conservative and reserved person," I explained. They assured me that all I needed was the desire to be filled with the Holy Spirit to receive the gift since I already had received Jesus Christ as my personal Lord and Savior. As they prayed, I wondered silently. "What is it going to feel like?" "Will I be scared?" "Can I really handle this?" Amidst all these questions, I still had doubt. The evangelists laid hands on me and before I knew what happened I heard a loud scream come from deep within me. I began to cry as I was filled with the Holy Spirit, as my spirit awakened from the dead and I began speaking in tongues.

Acts 8:17 KJV - Then laid they their hands on them, and they received the Holy Ghost.

Another year would pass before I would speak in tongues for the third time. This time I was visiting a cousin's Apostolic church. The minister had asked for those who needed prayer to come forth. Although I felt as though I should go forward, I did not move. The minister then came directly to me. The minister stated that I knew God wanted me to come forth for prayer. I went forward and as soon as he laid hands on me I began to speak in tongues.

Although I was a member of the Baptist faith for over ten

years, the Holy Spirit led me to take a spiritual class at an Apostolic church. The class was "Understanding the Master's Voice." I looked forward to taking the class. Hearing from God! While viewing the class outline, I noticed the subject of Spirit to spirit communication. Here was that subject again, "speaking in tongues." For some reason I still had fear. Although I had spoken in tongues three times before, it had never been one-to-one communication without intercession. I began praying at night before I went to bed to experience spirit to Spirit communication with the Lord. But nothing would happen and I was at a loss for my role in the oc-currence. I would pray and then I would silently wait for the Holy Spirit to do "His thing." I would await Him in fear with muscles tensed. I waited for the Holy Spirit holding on to self-control. Self control and indepen-dence – the two strongholds on my spirit. I had always held back a part of me in all situations (in friendships, in relationships, in all areas of my life). "If I let anyone get too close to me, they may hurt me." "I can't totally let go." Now, I was applying my life's philosophy sub-consciously to God. What nerve! How selfish! I was trying to keep a portion of myself away from my Creator. Of course, initially I did not realize what I was doing, but looking back it becomes all too clear. I waited on the Holy Spirit to manifest Himself upon me. But it was up to me! God gives us free will. Each one of us has the ability to make our own choices. Faith without works is dead! In order to move or speak, one has to make the effort to initiate the action. Speaking in tongues is no different. I decided to let go and submit to God.

It happened one night during class. Although there was a scheduled topic for lecture, the Holy Spirit led the instructor to have one of the church mothers speak to the class. Instead of a formal lecture, the church mother asked the class to stand, pray, and to speak spirit to Spirit with the Lord. It was at that point that I released my independent spirit and asked the Lord for the "true" communication with Him. This was the first time that the gift of tongues had come upon me without intercession. I was excited! This is what it feels like! I no longer had to ask or wonder. The voice came from deep within my being. The sound was like my voice, but with a different tone. The language was of that I had never known. It was initially like a pulling from my gut as my spirit began to speak. I gave in and freely received the gift of the Holy Spirit. Since that time I have been blessed with the gift of tongues on a continual basis. Finally, spirit to Spirit communication with God; I will never hold back again!

1 Corinthians 14:2 KJV - For he that speaketh in an unknown tongue speaketh not unto men, but unto God: for no man understandeth him; howbeit in the spirit he speaketh mysteries.

Romans 8:26-27 KJV - Likewise the Spirit also

helpeth our infirmities: for we know not what
we should pray for as we ought: but the Spirit itself
maketh intercession for us with groanings which
cannot be uttered. And he that searcheth the hearts
knoweth what is the mind of the Spirit, because
he maketh intercession for the saints according
to the will of God.

Anyone who has ever experienced the indescribable presence of the Lord through the Baptism of the Holy Spirit and the gift of speaking in tongues cannot doubt that Jesus Christ exists.

John 16:7, 13 KJV - Nevertheless I tell you the truth;
It is expedient for you that I go away: for if I go not
away, the Comforter will not come unto you; but if
I depart, I will send him unto you.
Howbeit when he, the Spirit of truth, is come, he
will guide you into all truth: for he shall not speak of
himself; but whatsoever he shall hear, that shall he
speak: and he will show you things to come.

For those who are wondering, speaking in tongues IS NOT a requirement to receive salvation. Neither is taking a class a requirement for speaking in tongues. This is a gift and CANNOT be taught! However, a class setting can teach you doctrine on the Baptism of the Holy Spirit and the gift of speaking in tongues. A class can also help you to release inhibitions and fear so that you can receive the gift. Just as a person can lead others to receive the gift of salvation, a person can lead others to receive the gift of speaking in tongues. This gift can also be obtained in the presence of just you and the Lord. All that is required is faith and the willingness to receive.

Chapter Five

Mixed Signals

ixed signals are a combination of different systems that result in a response. Both social values and spiritual values are systems that are part of our daily lives. Social values are the "acceptable" norms that are drafted by men and are allowed by society. These values drive actions for our interaction within our communities, ourselves, and with one another. Social values are based upon "popular opinion." Verbal and written communication of what is deemed acceptable is revealed through the Internet, on television, in magazines, in newspapers, and through our conversations. Spiritual or moral values pertain to fundamental principles of right conduct rather than on laws or customs. Spiritual values pertain to the spirit as the seat of moral character. The world's value system is one of mixed signals. One moment a moral issue that had once been taboo, is being embraced by the world in the next moment. Suddenly, the once forbidden issue becomes part of the norm. The world is fickle and if you continually attempt to fit into its moving target, you will become fickle too! The world favors doing sinful things discretely as long as it doesn't obviously hurt anyone or you don't get caught. "It's your thang do what you want to do" and "If it feels good do it" are mottos that fit the world's system. This independent nature of doing things sets you up for separation from God. Webster defines independent as "not influenced or controlled by others; thinking or acting for oneself; not depending or contingent upon something else; not relying on another for aid or support; refusing to be under obligation to others." Independence has its' place. However, there is a cost for every independent decision we make when we omit God from the equation. The consequences of disobedience can be devastating. Who would think that such a simple act of eating a piece of fruit could lead to iniquity (inherent sin) and eternal death?

Genesis 3: 9-19 KJV - And the Lord God called unto Adam, and said unto him, Where art thou? And he said, I heard thy voice in the garden, and I was afraid, because I was naked; and I hid myself. And he said, Who told thee that thou wast naked? Hast thou eaten of the tree, whereof I commanded thee that thou shouldest not eat? And the man said, The woman whom thou gavest to be with me, she gave me of the tree, and I did eat. And the Lord God said unto the woman, What is this that thou hast done? And the woman said, The serpent beguiled me, and I did eat. And the Lord God said unto the serpent, Because thou hast done this, thou art cursed above all cattle, and above every beast of the field; upon thou belly shalt thou go, and dust shalt thou eat all the days of thou life: And I will put enmity between thee and the woman, and between thy seed and her seed; it shall bruise thy head, and thou shalt bruise his heel. Unto the woman he said, I will greatly multiply thy sorrow and thy conception; in sorrow thou shalt bring forth children; and thy desire shall be to thy husband, and he shall rule over thee. And unto Adam he said, Because thou hast hearkened unto the voice of thy wife, and hast eaten of the tree, of which I commanded thee, saying, Thou shalt not eat of it: cursed is the ground for thy sake; in sorrow shalt thou eat of it all the days of thy life; Thorns also and thistles shall it bring forth to thee; and thou shalt eat the herb of the field; In the sweat of thy face shalt thou eat bread, till thou return unto the ground; for out of it wast thou taken: for dust thou art, and unto dust shalt thou return.

Romans 5:12 KJV – Wherefore, as by one man sin entered into the world, and death by sin; and so death passed upon all men, for that all have sinned:

It was not the act itself of eating the fruit, but the disobedience towards God that opened the way for sin and death to enter the world. Even the perceived "little" sins can open the door to catastrophic, life altering, consequences.

God has a purpose and a plan for our lives. People of the world's system seek to fulfill the desires of their heart first and foremost. Many build their lives leaving God as an afterthought. "After I have achieved a certain status, then I can devote my life to the things of God." "I am not ready to live a righteous life just yet." They reserve God for a time after they have already established their own agendas. As long as God is not totally eliminated, some people reason that their spiritual role is being fulfilled. They seek outward and visual manifestations – the things that can be seen, touched, or felt. But what happens in the in-between time? What happens while they are chasing "fool's gold?" I have a friend whose life I admired. This friend appeared to have it all – career, family, and material success. The friend made this statement to me concerning her life, "all that glitters is not gold." My friend was telling me that although her life appeared wonderful from the outside looking in, the truth was that her life was not wonderful at all. I would later discover that my friend's life was far from perfect.

We spend so much time running and searching for something or someone to fill the void in our lives that we miss what we already have inside. The spirit within us, once released to the will of God, brings the peace and joy that we were searching for all the time. How ironic to find that we already possess the real treasure. The treasure could not be seen or touched because it is of a spiritual nature. When you create your own life instead of entering into the Creator's plan for your life, there will always be something missing. No matter how much worldly success you achieve or possessions you attain, there will ultimately be a void that cannot be filled without God. When you get off the path that God has preordained for you there is a price to pay. The curse does not come without a cause. Some people wonder why bad things happen to "good" people.

James 1: 12-15 KJV - Blessed is the man that endureth temptation: for when he is tried, he shall receive the crown of life, which the Lord hath promised to them that love him. Let no man say when he is tempted, I am tempted of God: for God cannot be tempted with evil, neither tempteth he any man: But every man is tempted, when he is drawn away of his own lust, and enticed. Then when lust hath conceived, it bringeth forth sin: and sin, when it is finished, bringeth forth death.

Some reject Christianity because they do not want to be affiliated with a God who they perceive as allowing pain and suffering without intervening. Sorrow is a by-product of sin. Not one of us is without a sinful nature, be it of thought, word, or deed. The Bible tells us that there will be seasons of suffering as well as seasons of joy.

Ecclesiastes 3: 1, 4 KJV – To every thing there is a season, and a time to every purpose under the heaven:

A time to weep, and a time to laugh; a time to mourn, and a time to dance;

Remember Jesus Christ, who while on earth, was without sin and was subjected to pain and suffering. Why should we expect to escape?

Several people have asked me the difficult question, "What happens to people who have never had the opportunity to hear about Jesus, do they go to hell? The following scriptures speak to this question.

Romans 2: 12-16 AMP – All who have sinned without the Law will also perish without [regard to] the Law, and all who have sinned under the Law will be judged and condemned by the Law. For it is not merely hearing the Law [read] that makes one righteous before God, but it is the doers of the Law who will be held guiltless and acquitted and justified. When Gentiles who have not the [divine] Law do instinctively what the Law requires, they are a law to themselves, since they do not have the Law. They show that the essential requirements of the Law are written in their hearts and are operating there, with which their consciences (sense of right and wrong) also bear witness; and their [moral] decisions (their arguments of reason, their condemning or approving thoughts) will accuse or perhaps defend and excuse [them]. On that day when, as my Gospel proclaims, God by Jesus Christ will judge men in regard to the things which they conceal (their hidden thoughts).

Isaiah 52: 14-15 NIV – Just as there were many who were appalled at him – his appearance was so disfigured beyond that of any man and his form marred beyond human likeness – so will he sprinkle many nations, and kings will shut their mouths because of him. For what they were not told, they will see, and what they have not heard, they will understand.

Romans 15:21 KJV – But as it is written, To whom he was not spoken of, they shall see: and they that have not heard shall understand.

How do those who do not know of Jesus become aware of His existence and receive salvation? I personally do not know how this happens. The Bible provides various accounts of God speaking to people directly or indirectly through other people, visions or dreams. But, the

Word tells us that God is a faithful and just God (Deuteronomy 32:4). And, scripture tells us that God's Word is true (Psalm 33:4). Besides, who are we to question God on how He handles His business?

> Isaiah 29:16 NKJV – Surely you have things turned around! Shall the potter be esteemed as the clay; For shall the thing made say of him who made it, "He did not make me"? Or shall the thing formed say of him who formed it, "He has no understanding"?

God makes salvation available to all! God sacrificed His Son, Jesus, that all may spend eternity with Him. This is His greatest desire.

> John 3: 16-17 KJV – For God so loved the world, that he gave his only begotten Son, that whosoever believeth in him should not perish, but have everlasting life. For God sent not his Son into the world to condemn the world; but that the world through him might be saved.

In the world today many people believe in inclusion. The belief is that everyone should be able to live life openly any way they desire as long as it is "socially" legal. Inclusion of all life styles and ideology sounds good in theory, but what about the consequences. In the Bible, both, Aaron (the Priest) and King Saul paid a heavy price for giving in to the whims of the immoral majority.

Exodus 32: 1, 3-4 NIV - When the people saw that Moses was so long in coming down from the mountain, they gathered around Aaron and said, "Come, make us gods who will go before us. As for this fellow Moses who brought us up out of Egypt, we don't know what has happened to him."

So all the people took off their earrings and brought them to Aaron. He took what they handed him and made it into an idol cast in the shape of a calf, fashioning it with a tool. Then they said, "These are your gods, O Israel, who brought you up out of Egypt."

Exodus 32: 25, 35 NIV - Moses saw that the people were running wild and that Aaron had let them get out of control and so become a laughingstock to their enemies.

And the Lord struck the people with a plague because of what they did with the calf Aaron had made.

1 Samuel 15: 24 KJV - And Saul said unto Samuel, I have sinned: for I have transgressed the commandment of the Lord, and thy words: because I feared the people, and obeyed their voice.

We must be careful, for to include everyone's ideas and fantasies into mainstream society would ultimately lead to eternal death. God believes in inclusion, but not the way the world looks at it. God's Word states that He loves all His children for He created them and He wants the very best for them. But like any parent, God loves His children enough to tell them the truth. God has provided us with the Bible as a guideline on how to live in accordance to His Word.

2 Timothy 3:16 KJV - All scripture is given by inspiration of God, and is profitable for doctrine, for reproof, for correction, for instruction in righteousness:

God has an order for us to follow. Seek to do the things of God first. This doesn't mean that we should seek God only and abandon the world. Balance is required in our lives. An abundance of anything is not good when it is not taken in the proper perspective. You can hide yourself away from the world and selfishly commune with Him alone, but to do that would not be fulfilling God's purpose. Yes, God wants to fellowship with us, but He also put us on this earth to do a job. God wants us to work. He wants us to expand His kingdom on earth. How can we expand His kingdom if we are not seeking to bring the unsaved into His fold?

Some in the world see Christians as hypocrites and use this as an excuse to denounce Christianity. They have heard or viewed persons who profess themselves as Christian in unholy acts or who use the Bible to promote their own personal agendas. Don't use this as an excuse not to accept Christianity. God knows the heart and deals with each person individually. You cannot and should not let the lives of others decide your personal eternity. God is interested in your relationship with Him. Besides, that person caught in a sinful act or misusing God's Word does not represent the whole Christian faith. You owe it to yourself to find out the truth about Christianity. The truth will make you free! (John 8:32)

> **James 1:5-8 NIV** – If any of you lacks wisdom, he should ask God, who gives generously to all without finding fault, and it will be given to him. But when he asks, he must believe and not doubt, because he who doubts is like a wave of the sea, blown and tossed by the wind. That man should not think he will receive anything from the Lord; he is a double-minded man, unstable in all he does.

Some people accept Christianity, but have become disillusioned with churches. They feel that too many churches have lost the focus of God. They cite high profile churches and the material wealth of some pastors as their excuse for not attending church services. Do not mistake God's blessings for fraudulent behavior. It is true that some church leaders are less than honest and others who once were examples to their congregations have strayed from the course. The body of Christ has to remember that church leaders are human. They are not perfect and they all will make some mistakes or some decisions that one may find objectionable. The majority of church leaders are honest and far outnumber the dishonest. One should not give up on church altogether just because some churches lose God's vision. We should always pray for our churches and our church leaders to encourage, provide strength, and to keep them in God's will. It is also critical for us to be prayerful concerning our church selection. The church selection should not be thought of in the same way one decides to join a social club, although one can and should develop social relationships at church. The church is not a place to go to see and be seen. Nor should we attend a church just because our friends and families are part of the congregation. One should seek God's guidance before selecting a church home. After all, God created us and established the church for our spiritual growth and nourishment. Who better to know where we should worship?

Ephesians 4: 11-13 NIV – It was he who gave
some to be apostles, some to be prophets, some to
be evangelists, and some to be pastors and teachers,
to prepare God's people for works of service, so that
the body of Christ may be built up until we all reach
unity in the faith and in the knowledge of the Son
of God and become mature, attaining to the whole
measure of the fullness of Christ.

The mixture of social values with spiritual values results

in chaos and confusion. At times a social value is violated and results in a spiritual value also being violated. When you have committed a sin that violates both social and spiritual morals, there is no doubt, there is no question to ponder, whether your behavior is inappropriate. But, for the socially "acceptable sins," when the world's system considers you as "good" and condones your misbehavior, many neglect to acknowledge that their behavior in the eyes of God is wrong. "What harm is a little white lie?" "If I was to get rid of the evidence no one will ever know" "No one will know if you don't tell them." All of these statements are false. God knows and if no one else is seemingly hurt, God is hurt by our disobedience. The mixed signal condition is not only experienced by non-Christians. A lot of Christians also fall into this dilemma. They want to fit into both worlds – social and spiritual. These "lukewarm" individuals are caught in the middle because they fail to make a choice. But, God says He would rather you be hot or cold rather than lukewarm.

Revelation 3:15-16 NIV - I know your deeds, that you are neither cold nor hot. I wish you were either one or the other! So, because you are lukewarm -- neither hot nor cold -- I am about to spit you out of my mouth.

There are also those who are so "spiritual" that they lack compassion for those who are at a place where they used to be. Do not forget that the same God that loves you loves those who are lost. Let us not sit on our self-imposed spiritual thrones gossiping and judging others.

Ephesians 2:1-5 NIV - As for you, you were dead in your transgressions and sins, in which you used to live when you followed the ways of this world and of the ruler of the kingdom of the air, the spirit who is now at work in those who are disobedient. All of us also lived among them at one time, gratifying the cravings of our sinful nature and following its desires and thoughts. Like the rest, we were by nature objects of wrath. But because of his great love for us, God, who is rich in mercy, made us alive with Christ even when we were dead in transgressions -- it is by grace you have been saved.

Ephesians 2:8-9 AMP - For it is by free grace (God's unmerited favor) that you are saved (delivered from judgment and made partakers of Christ's salvation) through [your] faith. And this [salvation] is not of yourselves [of your own doing, it came not through your own striving], but it is the gift of God; Not because of works [not the fulfillment of the Law's demands], lest any man should boast. [It is not the result of what anyone can possibly do, so no one can pride himself in it or take glory to himself.]

When Christians see others in trouble we should either

approach them in love, pray for them, or both as the Spirit leads us knowing that not one of us is perfect. There are "Holy Cliques" like there are "Social Cliques." Neither isolating clique is of God. Such conduct is one of the reasons people reject Christianity. Christians are not only to receive the Gospel, but also to share it with others. We must be willing to share God's blessings. Thank God for allowing the "wrong people" availability into the kingdom of heaven through salvation. Otherwise, heaven would be a very desolate place.

God has placed an internal check and balance system in our spirits. When we are headed in the wrong direction, our inner spirit gives us a warning to make us aware that we are out of line or to alarm us of impending danger. Have you ever wondered how a toddler inherently knows when he or she has done something morally wrong before anyone has taught them? Or, have you ever noticed that right before you encounter danger, you get a feeling of discomfort on the inside. God has provided us with our own internal warning system through our spirit.

Job 32:8 NIV – But it is the spirit in a man, the breath of the Almighty, that gives him understanding.

God provides even more revelation when you receive the gifts of Salvation and the Holy Spirit.

John 16:13 KJV – Howbeit when he, the Spirit of truth, is come, he will guide you into all truth: for he shall not speak of himself; but whatsoever he shall hear, that shall he speak: and he will show you things to come.

Upon encountering a warning in your spirit, yield and proceed with caution, always keeping God foremost in your decisions and your choices. The Holy Spirit will give you the insight to either move forward or warn you not to proceed.

I once heard a theologian speak on the life of man. He stated that a person's tombstone is inscribed with their name, date of birth, and date of physical death. The dash between the dates represents the life of the individual. How are you spending your between time? Are you giving off mixed signals? Are you too hot (so spiritual that you lack the compassion to share the Gospel with the lost), too cold (your life is consumed with sinful acts and the ways of the world), or lukewarm (one foot in the ways of the world and one foot following the ways of God)? The sad thing about the lukewarm individuals is that most do not even have a clue that they are lost. But God is good and He leaves us with the opportunity to obtain knowledge and change. God's mercy and grace is available for us all, just for the asking.

Chapter Six

The Package
vs. The Gift

*G*od is a three-fold being— God the Father, God the Son (Jesus), and God the Holy Spirit. Man is also a three-fold being— spirit, soul, and body (1 Thessalonians 5:23). These three distinct phases of man each have its own purpose and is united to serve the will of God. Man is a spirit who lives in a body (the flesh) and possesses a soul.

Spirit - Our spiritual realm is that part of us that fellowships and communicates with God. The spirit man is our real person and is referred to in the Bible as the hidden man of the heart. God made man in His image to fellowship with Him. God is Spirit therefore man is spirit. And like God, the spirit man is eternal. The spirit man exists in the saved and the unsaved. As we are born again and accept Jesus Christ as our Lord and Savior, our spirit man is renewed. Our spirit is then born of God and we become new creatures in Him. The spirit man is that voice that you hear inside yourself (our conscience). Evil spirits and the Holy Spirit speak to our spirit man. Therefore, it is important to strengthen our spirit man so that we can distinguish what voice we are hearing. The voice of the Holy Spirit will always align with the Word of God (the Bible). You build up your spirit man by increasing your knowledge of the Word.

Soul - Our soul or our mental realm is our intellectual dimension that reasons, thinks, and deals with emotions. Our minds obtain worldly information daily through our conversations, what we read, what we see, and what we hear. We translate this information that we receive and we make decisions based upon it. But, what kind of information are we receiving and what are we doing with it? God holds us accountable for our inputs and our decisions (our outputs). Mental renewal takes place by reading and meditating on the Word of God and by being taught by spiritual teachers ordained by God.

Body - Our physical realm and outer appearance. This earthly nature of man, the body, is the phase humans know in daily existence. It's that part of us that you can see and touch. The body's purpose is to carry out God's work, perform our earthly functions, and to house our spirits. Because our bodies house our spirits we are to take special care of them and present them to God as a living sacrifice.

> **Romans 12:1 AMP** - I Appeal to you therefore,
> brethren, and beg of you in view of [all] the mercies
> of God, to make a decisive dedication of your bodies
> [presenting all your members, and faculties] as a living
> sacrifice, holy (devoted, consecrated) and well pleasing
> to God, which is your reasonable (rational, intelligent)
> service and spiritual worship.

> **2 Corinthians 4:7 KJV** - But we have this treasure in
> earthen vessels, that the excellency of the power may
> be of God, and not of us.

Most people, who have not renewed their minds, only believe what they see. But, earthly visions can be misleading. Deception and lies are earthly occurrences. What you see on the outside may not necessarily be the substance of the total package. We have to be careful and guard our physical sight.

The least of man's three-fold being is the body, the outer appearance. The independent spirit leads us to think that the outside is what counts. Our physical attributes are the first to be noticed. Therefore, many people tend to neglect their innermost self and work to perfect or better what the world sees. The spirit being is left inside the body trapped and ignored. This is out of the order of God. How we look and what we wear too often takes precedence over finding out who we really are and what truly is our life's purpose. There is nothing wrong with being fashionable, wearing make-up, or presenting ourselves to look our best. The problem comes when we focus our attention on the outer appearance and neglect our inner content. God has made each of us as part of His master plan. Each of us is special in His eyes. Each one of us has a destiny to fulfill. God designed a plan for us prior to our births.

Ephesians 2:10 AMP - For we are God's [own] handiwork (His workmanship), recreated in Christ Jesus, [born anew] that we may do those good works which God predestined (planned beforehand) for us [taking paths which He prepared ahead of time], that we should walk in them [living the good life which He prearranged and made ready for us to live].

I have been guilty and I am sure that many others also have judged a person from their outer appearance. If a person is well groomed and dressed in expensive clothing and jewelry, one typically believes that they have their life together. But do they? You have only seen the surface. Upon further examination you may find that your impression of the immaculate person is totally inaccurate. I remember years ago reading an article in a national magazine that stuck with me. The article was concerning a single woman executive. By the world's standards, the woman had it all together! She was a high-ranking executive in a Fortune 500 company with a six-figure salary. The woman executive had a designer wardrobe, an expensive car, and a home in an exclusive neighborhood. She was among the trendsetters on the social scene. The lady executive was at the top of the social ladder. But with everything worldly to live for, she took her own life. Why would someone with all that going for themself take their own life? I would read further to find out that the lady executive had been exposed, her life, as she knew it was ruined. The "perfect" package had been soiled. An envious co-worker had found out the lady executive's secret and revealed it to the authorities. The immaculate and talented lady executive had lied about her scholastic credentials on her job application. The lady executive had never graduated from college. The executive was aware that there was an investigation underway concerning her application and the life she had created would now be destroyed. She felt as though she had nothing to live for, so she took her own life.

The tragic story of the lady executive made me think about her focus. Outside perfection taking precedence over inner growth. The lady executive had spent so much time climbing the social ladder, however she neglected to release and advance her inner spirit. If only she had taken the time to discover the inner spirit, her true identity. If only she knew God accepts us as we are. If only she knew just how much God loved her. If only she knew that God gave his only begotten Son so that she could have eternal life. If only... But, instead she took her life that Jesus died for and in return risked eternal death.

1 Timothy 6:6-10 NKJV - Now godliness with contentment is great gain. For we brought nothing into this world, and it is certain we can carry nothing out. And having food and clothing, with these we shall be content. But those who desire to be rich fall into temptation and snare, and into many foolish and harmful lusts which drown men in destruction and perdition. For the love of money is a root of all kinds of evil, for which some have strayed from the faith in their greediness, and pierced themselves through with many sorrows.

Proverbs 14:12 KJV - There is a way which seemeth right to a man, but the end thereof are the ways of death.

God's Word tells us in Hosea 4:6 that people are destroyed for the lack of knowledge.

Through my experiences I have encountered people whose outer package (the wrapping) hid what was going on inside. People who seemed to have it all together have surprised me when later I would see them stumble and at times even fall. These people with independent spirits could not deal with the world seeing their failures so they retreated into themselves.

> **Proverbs 16:18 KJV** - Pride goeth before destruction,
> and an haughty spirit before a fall.

> **1 John 2:16 AMP** - For all that is in the world --
> the lust of the flesh [craving for sensual gratification]
> and the lust of the eyes [greedy longings of the mind]
> and the pride of life [assurance in one's own resources
> or in the stability of earthly things] -- these do not
> come from the Father but are from the world [itself].

I can understand the independent spirit because I once was an independent spirit. I know the pressure that exists when you have self-control instead of God control. Releasing control to anyone or anything seems unbearable because you leave yourself open to do and follow the person or thing that has control over you. You may not be able to control outside forces, your job, other people or situations. The one thing you can control, is yourself. With the loss of self-control and the lack of spiritual knowledge, one may feel that there is nothing left.

My package may have seemed together on the outside but the inner spirit was locked away waiting to be released. It was not until I received true salvation that I was able to let the independent spirit go and let Jesus Christ take His place as the head of my life. No longer was I taking control over my life and it was a relief! By releasing the spirit within, I received peace of mind and body.

> John 14: 27 TLB - "I am leaving you with a gift -- peace of mind and heart! And the peace I give isn't fragile like the peace the world gives. So don't be troubled or afraid.

Have you released your spirit? Is Jesus Christ the head of your life? Do you know where you will spend eternity? If you answered "no" or "I don't know" to the above questions, you can answer, "yes" to the questions without doubt. God has provided us with a gift, a free gift. God gives us free will. You can accept Him and His gift of salvation or you can reject the gift. The decision is yours. Receive the gift of salvation today.

Why is salvation required? Because of the fall of man (Adam) to sin, sin and death were passed onto all men.

> Romans 5:12 KJV - Wherefore, as by one man sin entered into the world, and death by sin; and so death passed upon all men, for that all have sinned:

God, in His mercy, provided a way out from eternal death with life everlasting.

> John 3: 16-17 KJV – For God so loved the world,

that he gave his only begotten Son, that whosoever believeth in him should not perish, but have everlasting life.

God's salvation can only be obtained through His Son, Jesus Christ.

John 14: 6 AMP – Jesus said to him, I am the Way and the Truth and the Life; no one comes to the Father except by (through) Me.

You can receive Jesus Christ as your personal Savior by believing in Him and asking Him to come into your heart (not the organ, but your inner most being). Why not give authority to the one who made the ultimate sacrifice (crucifixion) for your life? You've tried living your way, why not try living God's way? Receive the gift of salvation by saying the following prayer with conviction.

A Prayer of Salvation

Dear Heavenly Father, I believe that Jesus Christ
is the Son of God. I believe Jesus died for me on the cross
at Calvary bearing my sins. I believe Jesus was raised from
the dead and He is alive today. Dear Heavenly Father,
I repent of all my sins and ask your forgiveness.
I confess with my mouth and believe with my heart
that Jesus Christ is my personal Lord and Savior.
Therefore, I am born again.

Congratulations! If you read aloud the above prayer with belief in your heart, you have received salvation and have placed Jesus Christ as the head of your life. Old things are now passed away. Your spirit has been release You are now a new creation, born anew!

Romans 10: 9-10, 13 KJV - That if thou shalt confess with thy mouth the Lord Jesus, and shalt believe in thine heart that God hath raised him from the dead, thou shalt be saved. For with the heart man believeth unto righteousness; and with the mouth confession is made unto salvation.

For whosoever shall call upon the name of the Lord shall be saved.

2 Corinthians 5:17 KJV- Therefore if any man be in Christ, he is a new creature: old things are passed away; behold, all things are become new.

Did you not receive salvation? Do you not think that Jesus will accept you as you are because you are not a "good " person? Or, do you think that you are a "good" person and do not need salvation since you know based upon your deeds you have a reserved place in heaven waiting for you. If you answered in the affirmative to either of the above questions, then you are in for an awakening.

Ephesians 2: 8-9 KJV - For by grace are ye saved through faith; and that not of yourselves: it is the gift of God: Not of works, lest any man should boast.

The "good" person status does not automatically secure you a spot in heaven. Your denomination, religious rituals, or your status in the church won't save you. Nothing you can do (help the needy, sing in the choir, usher, deacon, or even pastor a church) guarantees you life everlasting. You can be a "good" person by the world's standards and not spend eternity with God. Entry into heaven is based upon the grace of God, not based upon your good works. Receive salvation and enter into God's kingdom. When you willingly refuse to receive salvation (eternal life), you are accepting eternal death (Deuteronomy 30:19). Given the two choices, why not accept life everlasting?

For those who feel that you need to wait until you get it together before dedicating yourself to God, don't you know that you need God to get your life together? God has accepted lots of misled people (those who were disobedient, liars, thieves, adulterers, and even murderers).

King David, a former shepherd boy who had been appointed king by God, saw Bathsheba (another man's wife) taking a bath and was tempted by the lust of his flesh. David sent for and slept with Bathsheba. Upon finding out that Bathsheba was with child, David sent Bathsheba's husband into battle where he would certainly be killed. Then David took Bathsheba as his bride.

2 Samuel 12: 9 KJV - Wherefore hast thou despised the commandment of the Lord, to do evil in his sight? thou hast killed Uriah the Hittite with the sword, and has taken his wife to be thy wife, and has slain him with the sword of the children of Ammon.

2 Samuel 12: 13 KJV - And David said unto Nathan, I have sinned against the Lord. And Nathan said unto David, The Lord also hath put away thy sin; thou shalt not die.

Rahab was a harlot (prostitute) who hid the men Joshua sent to spy Jericho. Because of her faithfulness to the men of God, Rahab, her possessions, and her father's household were spared when the city was set on fire.

Joshua 6: 24-26 KJV - And they burnt the city with fire, and all that was therein: only the silver, and the gold, and the vessels of brass and of iron, they put into the treasury of the house of the Lord. And Joshua saved Rahab the harlot alive, and her father's household, and all that she had; and she dwelleth in Israel even unto this day; because she hid the messengers, which Joshua sent to spy out Jericho.

The Apostle Paul, who was once known as Saul of Tarsus, threatened, tormented, and slaughtered disciples of Jesus. In the midst of Saul's evil doings, God entered Saul's life and turned his life around. Saul became Paul, God's chosen vessel who brought the Gentiles into Christianity.

Acts 9: 13-15 AMP- But Ananias answered, Lord, I have heard many people tell about this man, especially how much evil and what great suffering he has brought on Your saints at Jerusalem; Now he is here and has authority from the high priests to put in chains all who call upon Your name. But the Lord said to him, Go, for this man is a chosen instrument of Mine to bear My name before the Gentiles and kings and the descendants of Israel;

With God all things are possible (Matthew 19:26)! He is a God of second chances – multiple chances. God can take the most unlikely person and thrust them into greatness. God has not changed. He is the same yesterday, today, and forever (Hebrews 13:8). God is no respecter of persons. What He has done for others, He can do for you. He loves you. You are His creation. It is not too late. Go back and confess the prayer of salvation. Don't let Satan steal one more day of your life!

I hope you received Jesus Christ as your personal Lord and Savior. If you still failed to receive salvation, it's your life and your decision. You don't know when your time on earth will come to an end (Ecclesiastes 9:12). Tomorrow is not promised to anyone. Remember, God gives us free will. God is a gentleman. He will never force you to accept Him.

If you have confessed salvation in your past and have slipped back (back-slidden) into the world's system, confess your sins, repent and ask forgiveness of the Lord. Ask Him to protect you and to give you strength to walk away permanently from those things that are not pleasing to Him. Stay in prayer, God's Word, and attend regular church services at the church God directs. This will help you to maintain your strength and spiritual feeding.

1 John 1:9 KJV - If we confess our sins, he is faithful and just to forgive us our sins, and to cleanse us from all unrighteousness.

A Prayer of Rededication

Dear Heavenly Father, I confess the sin of (fill in the blank) and ask your forgiveness. Lord, I proclaim to remove myself from the temptation of (fill in the blank) in my life. I pray for strength over my weaknesses. I thank you for forgiving me and cleansing me from my sins. Today, I am back in right fellowship with you in the name of Jesus.

When you are in God's kingdom you will receive His promises and His rewards.

Renew your mind. Seek to find your purpose and God's role for your life. Learn to live a life that will be pleasing to God, not your flesh. Be not conformed to this world, but be transformed by the renewal of your mind.

Romans 12:2 AMP - Do not be conformed to this world (this age), [fashioned after and adapted to its external, superficial customs], but be transformed (changed) by the [entire] renewal of your mind [by its new ideas and its new attitude], so that you may prove [for yourselves] what is the good and acceptable and perfect will of God, even the thing which is good and acceptable and perfect [in His sight for you].

Read out loud the Word of God (The Bible) daily. This allows you to not only speak the Word, but you will also hear the Word. You may want to incorporate the Bible books of Psalm (worship and praise) and Proverbs (wisdom and knowledge) into your daily devotion.

Proverbs 4:7 KJV - Wisdom is the principal thing; therefore get wisdom: and with all thy getting get understanding.

Don't get discouraged if at first when you begin reading the Bible you don't receive total understanding of what you read. Like most things, the more time you spend in the Word, the more you will be able to comprehend and the more the Spirit will reveal to you. A Concordance and a Key Word Study Bible are good tools to aid you in your study. Be sure to keep a dictionary available.

2 Timothy 3:16,17 AMP - Every Scripture is God-breathed (given by His inspiration) and profitable for instruction, for reproof and conviction of sin, for correction of error and discipline in obedience, [and] for training in righteousness (in holy living, in conformity to God's will in thought, purpose, and action), So that the man of God may be complete and proficient, well fitted and thoroughly equipped for every good work.

Do the Word. Be not only hearers of the word, but doers also. Don't just read the Bible, live the Bible. Faith without works is dead! The same faith that enabled you to receive salvation can be used in other areas of your life.

Seek a church home. Pray and ask God to lead you where He wants you to serve. Don't limit your search to a certain denomination or certain membership size. No church is too small or too large when it comes to the Lord's direction. Neither should you select a church based upon the length of the service. Be open to hear from God. He will place you in a church that will help you to grow spiritually and enable you to become a benefit to the congregation. As you visit different churches during your search, you will eventually find the church for you. How will you know? You will know by the peace that you will feel in your spirit. Pray and ask God to confirm your church selection. Then, pray and ask God where He would have you to serve in your new church home.

Fellowship with those who are like-minded. This may mean that you will have to let go of some relationships. The relationships that cause you to drift toward your old habits may need to be severed. Some old relationships will grow as you walk forward together or are led in the same spiritual direction. New relationships will develop when you walk in your purpose.

I pray that you have received your free gift and released your spirit from within so God's will for your life can now be revealed.

Ephesians 1:13-19 KJV - In whom ye also trusted, after that ye heard the word of truth, the gospel of your salvation: in whom also after that ye believed, ye were sealed with that holy Spirit of promise. Which is the earnest of our inheritance until the redemption of the purchased possession, unto the praise of his glory. Wherefore I also, after I heard of your faith in the Lord Jesus, and love unto all the saints, Cease not to give thanks for you, making mention of you in my prayers;

That the God of our Lord Jesus Christ, the Father of glory, may give unto you the spirit of wisdom and revelation in the knowledge of him: The eyes of your understanding being enlightened; that ye may know what is the hope of his calling, and what the riches of the glory of his inheritance in the saints, And what is the exceeding greatness of his power to us-ward who believe, according to the working of his mighty power.

About the Author

Robin L. Anderson was born and raised in Detroit, Michigan. Robin received a Bachelor of Science degree in Biochemistry and a Master of Science degree in Industrial Engineering. She is currently pursuing her God-given purpose. Upon her spiritual awakening, Robin had a strong desire to seek the deeper things of God. This led to her completion of Catechism, Laypersons, and Kingdom Business studies. Robin was divinely inspired to share her spiritual journey in her debut book, **Out of the Box - Releasing the Spirit Within**. Robin L. Anderson is the founder of Shining Light Works with the mission to share the revelations of God by providing "good works".

Matthew 5:16 NKJ - Let your light so shine before men, that they may see your good works and glorify your Father in heaven.

To contact Robin L. Anderson or to order additional copies of this book, visit the following website:

www.shininglightworks.com

or send correspondence to:

Shining Light Works
P.O. Box 1072
Farmington, Michigan 48333